War Birds

Published in 1984 by Osprey Publishing Limited
12–14 Long Acre, London WC2E 9LP
Member company of the George Philip Group

British Library Cataloguing in Publication Data

Jerram, Mike
    Warbirds.—(Osprey colour series)
    1. Fighter planes—History   2. World War,
    1939–1945—Aerial operations
    I. Title
    623.74'64'09044   UG1242.F5

ISBN 0-85045-578-2

Editor Dennis Baldry
Printed in Hong Kong

War Birds

Mike Jerram

Contents

Mike Jerram's earliest recollection of warbirds is of watching Fleet Air Arm Fireflies, Sea Furies and Sea Hornets landing at Lee-on-Solent. Although his work as a freelance aviation writer and photographer brings him into contact with every kind of flying machine from microlights to the Space Shuttle, he has a particular passion for vintage aircraft and warbirds and has spent many years photographing them, not entirely without incident. Two trips in a B-17G Fortress were both punctuated by tailwheel failures, the first when the bomber was at the end of its display slot and the Red Arrows were due on next. Jerram was delegated to go back to the tail cone to investigate the recalcitrant wheel's apparent failure to extend. No-one told him they carried a spare wheel back there . . . On another occasion while shooting close to the active runway at an American airshow he committed the cardinal sin of the action photographer and turned his back on his subjects to reload cameras. A sudden change in engine note and a screech of protesting rubber focussed attention, but not cameras, just as the Corsair pilot managed to tame his ground loop a few yards from the petrified photographer.

Aged 38, Mike Jerram lives and works on the south coast. He is contributing editor of the British general aviation magazine *Pilot* and an assistant compiler of *Jane's All the World's Aircraft*.

To my wife, Kaye.

In the mid-1960s the production team of the great movie epic *The Battle of Britain* were greatly surprised to discover that the Royal Air Force was quite unable to supply squadrons of Spitfires and Hurricanes to take part in recreating that desperate aerial combat of 1940. A few Spitfires were available, but only one Hurricane was flying in Britain and nowhere, *nowhere* could be found a genuine airworthy Luftwaffe aircraft.

In Britain, and to much the same extent in the United States, the historic warplanes of the last world war had been junked by the thousand in peacetime, some types lost forever to the breakers' cutting torches. The good folk who willingly gave their saucepans for Spitfires in time of national need soon had their cookware back a hundredfold. To this uncaring destruction were sacrificed the last complete examples of Whitley, Hampden, Halifax and Stirling bombers a quarter century or more ago.

Happily there is today a greater awareness of the value of such treasures, and that awareness is being channelled not just to static preservation in museums, laudable though many of them are, but to the maintenance and creation of airworthy aircraft of WW II – warbirds.

What is a warbird? There is no positive definition, but broadly speaking the term is applied to aircraft which served in WW II or in the immediate post-war period, including the Korean War. In *Warbirds* you will find some aircraft which stretch that definition a little, others which played supporting roles in battle but had neither the weaponry nor stamina to act as aggressors. They are all part of the warbird movement, and welcome. Few but the best-heeled can aspire to own and operate a Spitfire or a P-51, whose price tags (when they come on the market but rarely) run to six figures. But a Piper Cub costs no more, and often less, than a saloon car, and has equal claim to wear a uniform.

Thanks to dedicated groups such as the Battle of Britain Memorial Flight, Warbirds of America and the Confederate Air Force, the warbird movement is not only alive and well, but thriving internationally. Long-forgotten aircraft are being sought out in the obscurer parts of the world where they were cast off by air forces on the way to better things, and painstakingly restored to their rightful place: in the air. If you wonder why, take a careful look at the crowd at the next major airshow you visit. While some people will be captivated by the deafening afterburner roar and now-you-see-it-now-you-don't lightning quick dashes of 1980s jet fighters, and others will dwell on every twist and turn of buzzing, bee-like Pitts Specials, the only sight and sound *guaranteed* to get everyone's head out of their programme or feet out of the refreshment tent is that of a WW II fighter or bomber. It is more than nostalgia, for many of those so moved have parents too young to remember the days when these aircraft were the last word in military sophistication. And that, perhaps, is the key to the warbird's charisma. It represents the combat aircraft and pilot at their purest, man and machine unfettered by the electronic gadgetry of modern push-button fire and forget warfare. In these warplanes you really *can* get to see the whites of the pilot's eyes.

Mike Jerram
Southsea, Hampshire
March 1984

Wild horses

Mustang: the fiery wild horse of the American prairie. Ironically both the inscription for the classic fighter and its name came from Britain, not the United States, after the British Purchasing Commission gave the North American Aviation company just four months to design and build a new fighter for the Royal Air Force in 1940. P-51D pictured here was the definitive Mustang, powered by a Packard-built Rolls-Royce Merlin engine delivering 1695 hp. Earlier Allison engined-Mustangs lacked puff at high altitude and were relegated to tactical reconnaissance duties with the RAF, but the P-51D could top 41,000 ft and reach 438 mph. With drop tanks the Mustang's fuel load gave it very long legs, enabling it to fly bomber escort on round trip missions of 1500 miles and more

Off and running John Baugh's P-51D *Miss Coronado* was once the mount of famed North American Rockwell test pilot and airshow performer Bob Hoover. Removal of fuselage fuel tank, armour plate and military radio gear leaves room aplenty for two under the Mustang's bubble top canopy

Below Bill Clark squeaks his P-51D *Dolly* onto the runway at Oshkosh, Wisconsin for a one wheel landing at the end of a Warbirds of America mission, and runs up Old Glory on the way back to his parking slot

Like their four legged counterparts P-51s need plenty of grooming, but at least they don't kick. Scott Smith's P-51D is as slick as they come, with wet-look black and white paint and a red leather interior, yet. He calls it *Ge Ge II*. Some horse

Overleaf Los Angeles newspaper magnate Howard Keefe races his clip-wing P-51D *Miss America*. His Packard-Merlin has been tweaked up to produce more than 2,000 hp. Note also the Hoerner wingtips and low profile tinted canopy. *Miss America* caused hearts to flutter in more ways than one in 1970 when a runaway rudder trim tab jammed hard over when Keefe was boring down the straightaway at Reno at 450 mph during the Harrah's Trophy unlimited race. Keefe chopped the power as the Mustang skidded towards the grandstand and managed to bring the runaway to heel

Above Latin America has been a rewarding hunting ground for warbirds collectors, Mustang-lovers in particular, since many small air forces continued to operate them into the 1970s and one – the Dominican Air Force – still flies P-51Ds. *El Gato Rapido* came from the Costa Rican Air Force in 1978 and is pictured here after arrival in the United States

Six .50 machine guns were standard P-51D armament, used to good effect by Lieutenant Claiborne H Kinnard Jnr of Franklin, Tennessee who became an eight-victory ace while flying the original *Man O'War* with the 4th Fighter Group of the Eighth Air Force in England. Latter-day *Man O'War* has sixteen swastika 'kill' markings along the canopy rail

The P-51D's clear bubble canopy was one of the first of its kind for fighter aircraft, developed to improve combat visibility. Earlier P-51B and 'C models had heavy-framed 'razorback' canopies which severely limited the pilot's vision, especially to the rear. The British developed a bulged canopy called the Malcolm Hood which went part way to solving the problem, but North American Aviation drew on moulding techniques used for manufacturing glazed nose transparencies for bombers to develop the bubble top capable of withstanding flight speeds approaching 500 mph and rapid temperature changes during combat manouevring from high altitude. Pilots loved the bubble's near-perfect vision, were less pleased that it turned the cockpit into a hothouse in bright sunlight

Left Mustang at the gallop: *Passion Wagon* on the roll with the Merlin producing 1490 hp at 61 in of boost and the eleven foot Hamilton Standard paddle-bladed propeller tearing out chunks of air at 3000 rpm. Canadian Mustang below is just settling on its landing gear, the Merlin giving its characteristic snap-crackle-pop as it is throttled back. The Royal Canadian Air Force equipped with P-51Ds in 1947, and flew them with auxiliary squadrons until 1956

Below and Overleaf *Cottonmouth* is finished in the colours of a Mustang IV (the British Commonwealth always insisted on their own designations for American-built aircraft) serving with No 3 Sqn Royal Australian Air Force operating out of Zarro, Yugoslavia at the end of WW II

North American developed a lightweight version of the Mustang in an attempt to improve high speed performance and manoeuvrability without employing a bigger engine. The production version of the lightweight craft was designated P-51H. With a water-injected Packard V-1650-9 engine putting out a maximum 2218 hp the '51H could reach 487 mph at 25,000 ft and was the fastest of all production variants. P-51Hs, identifiable by the deeper, slightly longer fuselage, taller fin and rudder and small wheels, saw only limited war service in the Pacific shortly before the Japanese surrender, but were flown by USAF and Air National Guard units in peacetime. Five hundred and fifty-five were built, but few survive. This rare airworthy example is finished in the colours of the single aircraft supplied to the Royal Air Force for evaluation. The remarkable development of the P-51 is no better illustrated than by the P-51H's performance – fully 100 mph faster than the first Mustangs, which predated it by little more than three years

24

'Pope Paul I', alias Experimental Aircraft Association president Paul Poberezny, flies this Cavalier conversion of the P-51D at airshows and on business trips for the EAA. Cavalier Corporation of Sarasota, Florida, specialized in civilian conversions of P-51Ds, outfitting them with two-seat cockpits with modern instrument panels and avionics, baggage lockers in the wing gun/ammunition bays and a wide choice of fuel tankage offering up to 2000 miles range. At 400 mph plus the Mustang is a swift, if less than roomy cross-country carriage for those who like to arrive with more style than your mass-production Wichita wonder can offer. Poberezny tall-finned Cavalier Mustang wears the distinctive colour scheme of *Lou IV*, a P-51D flown by 361st Fighter Group commander Colonel T J J Christian Jr. The 361st called themselves *The Yellowjackets* hence the yellow cowling and spinner. Until recently the EAA also flew the oldest surviving Mustang, a prototype XP-51 Apache dating from 1941 which was the fourth aircraft built by North American. Now retired from active duty, it is displayed at the EAA Museum of Flight at Oshkosh

Mission completed. *Passion Wagon* rests as the sun goes down on another day in the long life of a fighter whose inauspicious beginnings could scarcely have heralded the Mustang's eventual emergence as the best Allied combat aircraft of WW II

Call it *Able Dog*, *Spad*, Skyraider or what you will, Douglas's AD attack aircraft is a big brute of an aeroplane which someone once said could carry everything but the kitchen sink . . . Pilots from US Navy attack squadron VA-195 proved that wrong when they raided the ablutions aboard USS *Princeton*, slung a cast iron sink from a 2000 lb bomb, and dropped the lot on a Communist position during the Korean War. The Skyraider, whose basic design was drafted by Ed Heinemann on butcher paper in a room at the Statler Hotel in Washington one 1944 night to meet a Navy Bureau deadline for contract submissions, was too late for WW II but served with distinction in attack, dive-bomber and early warning roles with the navy in Korea and was resurrected for use in Vietnam because of its prodigious weapons carrying capability and ability to absorb horrendous groundfire while remaining in the air – something sophisticated modern jets could seldom manage

Heavy metal

This beautifully restored Spad is actually a former US Navy AD-4N ECM aircraft, masquerading as an A-1H of VA-176, *The Thunderbolts*. During the Vietnam War an A-1H from VA-176 operating off of the USS *Intrepid* and flown by Lt Jg W Thomas Patton and Lt Peter Russell shot down a North Vietnamese MiG-17 jet fighter

Dedication on CWH FG-1D is to Lt
Robert Hampton Gray of the Royal Canadian
Volunteer Reserve who was awarded a posthumous
Victoria Cross for pressing home an attack on a
Japanese destroyer in the Bay of Onagawa on 9 August
1945 despite repeated flak hits. Gray crashed into the
sea just as the destroyer sank as a result of his bombing

Chance Vought's Corsair naval fighter earned the nickname bent-winged bird because of its unusual wing configuration, designed to enable short undercarriage legs to be used while still providing adequate ground/deck clearance for the 2000 hp Pratt & Whitney Double Wasp's massive propeller. About to touch down here is a Goodyear-built FG-1D Corsair owned by the Canadian Warplane Heritage. CWH president Dennis Bradley bought it, with just 1600 hours on the airframe and 300 on the engine, for $25,000

Above The F4U-5N Corsair was a night-fighter used throughout the Korean War. This restored example, lacking only the '5N's radome normally mounted on the starboard wing, wears the colours of *The Flying Nightmares* – Marines squadron VMF (N) 513. Lt Guy Bordelon, an F4U-5N pilot with US Navy squadron VC-3, became the only Navy ace of the Korean War with four Communist YAK-18s and one LA-2 downed

31

You can tell why the little guy was always the ball turret gunner in any Flying Fortress crew. Hunched, embryo style on a bicycle-saddle seat and sighting his twin .50s through his raised legs, his was the bomber's most important and seemingly most vulnerable defensive position, yet statistically proved the safest crew station in combat. Other crewmembers had to wind the turret up into the fuselage to enable the ball gunner to leave his cramped quarters, which tended to get piled knee deep in spent cartridge cases when things got hot

12,751 B-17 Flying Fortresses were built, of which more than one third were lost in wartime combat. Today only a handful survive in airworthy condition, mostly as flying museum pieces, though a few fly cargo in Latin America or dump quenching borate on forest fires in the United States. This B-17G is owned by the EAA Air Museum and scarcely lives up to its name, lacking the turrets and 13 .50 calibre machine guns which provided the Fortess's defences

Above The guns aren't real but *Sally B*, the only airworthy B-17 in Europe, looks convincing thanks to a TV company which financed some aluminium-and-fibreglass turrets for a movie role. This B-17G saw no active war service, but flew as a high altitude photo ship for the French government's mapping service until the British-based Eighth Air Force Memorial Flight acquired it as a flying tribute to the 79,000 American airmen who died over Europe in WW II

Big friends, little friends. A pair of P-51D Mustangs provide top cover for two B-17Gs just like it was back in '44. No steaming contrails here though, no marauding Luftwaffe fighters, no flak, just nostalgia and the blood-quickening note of eight Wright Cyclones and a pair of Rolls-Royce Merlins, around 14,000 hp in close formation

Right Wrights a-rumbling, crew watching the wingtips, the EAA's B-17G *Aluminum Overcast* eases out of a tight parking spot for a fly-by spot at the annual Fly-In and Convention at Oshkosh

That's how·they do things in Texas, with more . . . well, *pizzazz*. The Confederate Air Force's B-17F *Texas Raiders* taxies out with Old Glory and the flag of the Lone Star state sharing honours from the flight deck windows, and returns for a battle-damaged one wheel up, one wheel down touch and go which deservedly gets the good ole boys a round of applause, even from Damn Yankees. Just wait until they try a belly landing . . .

Germans called it *Der Gabelschwanz Teufel* – fork-tailed devil. The French said *Double Queue* – twin tailed one. The Japanese had a symbol for it meaning two aeroplanes, one pilot. The British and Americans called it simply Lightning. Whichever you prefer, Lockheed's P-38 was an innovative aeroplane: the first twin boom fighter; first with tricycle landing gear; first with turbo-supercharged engines; the first twin-engine, single-seat interceptor; the first to make extensive use of stainless steel in its airframe . . . You get the picture. The P-38 was a product of Lockheed's legendary designer Clarence 'Kelly' Johnson, who later directed the design of the P-80 Shooting Star, F-104 Starfighter, U-2 spyplane and the SR-71 Blackbird. Lightnings are rare birds indeed; this pristine example is a P-38L owned by Bill Ross of Lake Barrington Shores, Illinois

Nose art was a popular morale booster among USAAF crews in WW II. A good squadron artist could earn $15 a time for painting some curvaceous features on the side of an aeroplane. Many of the illustrations were inspired by Alberto Varga's dream-perfect girls from *Esquire*. When they got a little too revealing the top brass tried to impose censorship – after all, what would the folks back home think when they saw the publicity pictures – but cunning artists could soon apply a swimsuit or bikini. In washable paint, naturally. Sooner or later you could always depend on rain in Britain. *Miami Clipper*, here seen on a B-25 Mitchell, was

originally the heart-throb of a 91st Bomb Group B-17 crew based at Bassingbourn, England in 1944

Named after the US Army's controversial and court-martialled champion of air power General William 'Billy' Mitchell, the North American B-25 was widely used by the Allies in every war theatre and immortalized by Jimmy Doolittle's April 1942 raid on Tokyo when Mitchells attacked the Japanese capital after taking off from the aircraft carrier USS *Hornet*. Out to grass here are five Mitchells ferried across the Atlantic to Britain in 1977 for the film *Hanover Street*

Overleaf Gear coming up, Canadian Warplane Heritage's B-25J climbs away immaculate in the colours of No 98 Sqn Royal Canadian Air Force. After many years as an executive transport and avionics demonstration aircraft with the Bendix Corporation the CWH flagship was bought for $12,000, fully restored to military configuration as a Mitchell III and is the Collection's most popular performer. It is one of two Mitchells in the CWH fleet which is based at Hamilton, Ontario

Grumman's unique Sto-Wing mechanism put the aircraft's wings flush alongside the fuselage for maximum space saving in cramped aircraft carrier hangars and deck parking spots. Here Dick Dieter's General Motors built TBM-3R Avenger torpedo bomber does a fine impression of a pelican tucking up its wings. Huge greenhouse canopy and portly fuselage stripped of military hardware enables Dieter, from South Bend, Indiana, to be generous with joyrides for friends, as many as seven at a time

Nearly half a century after its first flight the perennial
Douglas DC-3 soldiers on with cargo haulers and air
forces the world over. Few are as lovingly cared for as
Tom Thomas Jr's C-53 transport in US Army Air
Corps colours pictured here after arrival at a Warbirds
of America gathering in Wisconsin after a trip from its
Oklahoma City base

Bad guys

'Why does that airplane look like that, mummy?'
'Because it's old and wrinkled like me.' No, they were
built that way, earning the Junkers JU-52/3M tri-
motor transport the well-deserved nickname *Iron Annie*.
This corrugated wonder is actually a Spanish-built
CASA 352. 170 *Tante Jus* were manufactured in Spain
and remained in service until the 1970s when the
survivors were eagerly snapped up by warbirds
collectors. Englishman Doug Arnold owns five,
including this one, and has a hangerful of spares for
the flying nissen huts

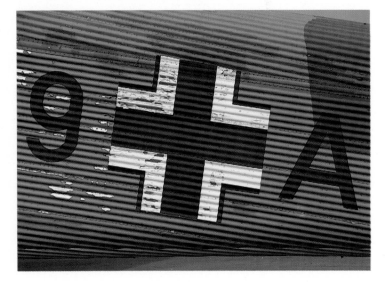

50

Thick section high-lift wing with full-span ailerons and slotted flaps characterize the Ju-52/3M. The Junkers-developed 'double wing' concept bestowed remarkable STOL performance and slow flight capability on the aircraft, but could be troublesome in bad weather when ice tended to accumulate in the gap between the surfaces leading to rapid loss of control. The corrugated airframe had legendary strength: one Luftwaffe pilot allegedly landed his *Tante Ju* on a tree-lined road and taxied for two miles smashing down trees to clear a path for following aircraft

Below Aptly-named Fieseler Storch (this one is a French-built Morane MS.500) was another slow flier which could manage a near hover in a modest breeze. Difficult to fly, with little natural stability and poorly harmonized controls, the Storch was nonetheless a remarkable performer in capable hands. SS Hauptsturmführer Otto Skorzeny organized a rescue mission for the Italian dictator Benito Mussolini in September 1943 using a Storch to pluck *Il Duce* from incarceration on a peak of the Gran Sasso Massif, more than 9000 ft up and accessible only by cable car. The Storch landed on a 200-yard rock-strewn strip on the side of the mountain. French-built aircraft like this one switched to metal-framed wings rather than wood after occupying Germans discovered French patriots sabotaging the aircraft by relieving themselves into the glue which held the wings together . . .

Although more than 33,000 were built, no genuine German-manufactured Messerschmitt Bf109 survives in airworthy condition. This imposter owned by the Confederate Air Force is a Spanish-built Hispano HA-1112 powered by a British-built Rolls-Royce Merlin engine. Twenty-eight HA-1112s were gathered together for the film *The Battle of Britain* and many have since been dispersed among museums and private collections in England and the United States. The CAF has four of them, this one bearing the markings of a Luftwaffe unit serving on the Eastern Front

Below Carl Bücker's classic aerobatic Jungmeister biplane is best remembered as the mount of Count Otto von Hagenburg, Alex Papana, Jose Aresti and Prince Constantin Cantacuzene, but was also used by the Luftwaffe for pilot training. Perfectly harmonized controls, fingertip response so light and precise that any manoeuvre could be started or stopped with pinpoint exactness, made the Jungmeister ideal for sharpening the reflexes of would-be fighter pilots, and much prized among collectors today. This example flying in England is unusual in having a Luftwaffe *Jagdfliegerschule* colour scheme

Whenever there is a need for newsreel footage of the wartime Blitz of London British television trots out an obviously faked sequence in which the fire-torn capital is viewed through a greenhouse much like this one on a Spanish-built Heinkel He III bomber. All that glassware afforded little protection for the crew and hampered rather than aided visibility, with distracting reflections bouncing back and forth from its many-faceted surfaces. So appalling was the cockpit visibility in bad weather that some variants of the Heinkel had a means of raising seat and control column to enable the pilot to poke his head through an opening roof panel for landing. The He III was the first modern bomber to enter Luftwaffe service, its 200 mph plus top speed leading Hermann Göring to conclude erroneously that it might outrun interceptors by fleet of foot alone. The He IIIs which spearheaded the Blitz were thus poorly defended and fell easy prey to RAF Hurricanes and Spitfires in daylight. More than 7000 were built, including 200 by CASA in Spain, whose last production CASA 2111 left the factory as late as 1956. This aeroplane, powered by a pair of Rolls-Royce Merlins in place of the original Daimler-Benz or Junkers Jumo engines, was ferried to England in 1978 and later sold to the Confederate Air Force at Harlingen, Texas

Cats and Hawks

Left Awkward, narrow-track 'roller skate' landing gear on this Wildcat became a Grumman hallmark after its introduction on the 1931 FF-1 biplane fighter, but was an invention of the Loening company, for which Grumman founder Leroy Grumman, Leon Swirbul and Bill Schwendler had worked. The Wildcat was conceived as a biplane, but emerged as the USN's first modern fighter. This aeroplane, owned by Joe Frasca, is a late production FM-2 model built by General Motors. That landing gear was hand-cranked, 29 turns to retract it, and was a sure give-away for a newcomer to the type because the cranking motion would transmit to his stick hand resulting in an undulating flight path after take-off until the gear was up

Above Pugnacious nose profile of the Curtiss P-40 inspired the much-imitated shark-mouth decoration shown on this P-40N owned by Suzanne Parish of Kalamazoo, Michigan

'Trust a woman to pick a colour like that!' observed a bystander when Suzanne Parish arrived at Oshkosh in her boudoir pink Curtiss P-40N. Not fair, sir. Though perhaps a trifle garish to the purist, the colour scheme represents the desert sand shade applied to USAAF aircraft during the North African campaign which bleached and weathered to a dusty pink hue. The P-40N Warhawk was the final production version of the Curtiss fighter. With a 1200 hp Allison V-1710-81 engine it had a maximum speed of 343 mph and carried six .50 machine guns. The last aircraft left the assembly line in December 1944 after 13,738 P-40s had been built

Hickham Field, Hawaii, December 7 1941. USAAC P-40s are caught on the ground as the first Japanese bombs explode during the attack on Pearl Harbor. Relax, it is just a realistic recreation of the Day of Infamy courtesy of the ordnance experts of the Confederate Air Force

Above Leaping tiger insignia on Rudy Frasca's P-40E was carried by aircraft of General Claire Lee Chennault's American Volunteer Group *Flying Tigers* flying against the Japanese out of Burma in the summer of 1941. In six months of operations the American mercenaries, who were each paid $700 a month for their services, destroyed 286 Japanese aircraft in aerial combat and 240 on the ground for the loss of 16 of their own. Though often characterized as a bunch of unruly mavericks, the AVG pilots honed themselves into a fine fighting force which used superior tactics to overcome the P-40's inferiority to Japanese fighters and strike sienificant blows with often as few as 20 airworthy aircraft on hand

The P-40, though inferior to most of its contemporaries, was the only 'modern' fighter in the American inventory when the United States went to war with the Japanese, yet paradoxically it remained in production until the end of 1944, long after more advanced types such as the P-51 Mustang were available. Why? Ability to absorb punishment and still come home was one reason, eloquently encapsulated by one P-40 pilot who declared that his aeroplane came back from missions 'so full of holes you had to put it against a dark background to see it'

Overleaf Grumman's F8F Bearcat was the last of the great 'cat' single engined fighters. This F8F-2 carries the markings of VF-11 *Red Rippers*, one of the oldest US Navy fighter squadrons, now flying F-14A Tomcats. VF-11's insignia on the cowling depicts a wild boar's head (taken from a gin bottle label), some baloney, two red balls and a lightning bolt. Students of heraldry will interpret this as meaning gin drunken, baloney slinging, fast moving bastards . . . Although it was photographed in the United States, this Bearcat is now based in Europe with British collector Stephen Gray

The Bearcat was a successful attempt to combine massive power with a small airframe to provide climb and roll rates twice those of its predecessor the F6F Hellcat. The 2800 hp Pratt & Whitney R-2800-34W Double Wasp engine gave this hot rod a climb rate of 5600 ft per minute and a maximum speed in later versions of 450 mph. One novel feature of the F8F-1 were its 'safety' wingtips, which featured expendable outer panels which were supposed to shear off by means of explosive bolts if the wing was overstressed by excessive G loads during high speed manoeuvring. Asymmetric departures of wingtips resulting in roll rates even more spectacular than usual killed that enterprising idea. The Bearcat arrived on the scene too late to see active service, but was used for ground-attack missions by the French in Indo China. The Bearcat pictured here is an immaculately restored F8F-2 wearing the colours of the Naval Reserve Air Center, Denver, Colorado

Brits, Spits, and bits

Remarkably young RAF pilots often found themselves in the cockpit of a Spitfire after too few hours in the less sophisticated Tiger Moth trainer. Both aircraft are classics of their kind, the Tiger Moth gentle and forgiving, but with a knack of emphasizing every sloppy piloting habit, the Spitfire slippery and knife-sharp with handling rarely matched and joyously rewarding to the skilled touch

Overleaf The de Havilland Tiger Moth was cobbled together from parts of other Moths to meet a British Air Ministry specification in 1931, and developed into one of the world's best-known training biplanes. Surplus Tigers sold post-war for £50 apiece; restored examples such as this one bearing wartime training camouflage now carry price tags of £20,000 or more

'Just the sort of bloody silly name they would choose,' sniffed designer Reginald Mitchell when told of the British Air Ministry's choice of Spitfire for his new fighter. Mitchell died before the aircraft entered RAF service and could scarcely have guessed the impact which his aeroplane was to have on world history, or the affection with which it is remembered. The Mark IX above is arguably the best-handling of all marks of Spitfire. This one, owned by a consortium led by former Red Arrows team leader Ray Hanna, fetched £260,000 at an auction in 1983 and is preserved in fully aerobatic condition

Right Instantly recognizable elliptical wing planform of the Spitfire is an aesthetic delight and a manufacturing headache. Unlike its simple 1920s-technology contemporary the Hawker Hurricane, the Spitfire, with its stressed skin monocoque fuselage, complex curvatures and subtlety of line, was ill-suited to the kind of mass production which was necessary in wartime. It has been estimated that each Spitfire took about 330,000 man hours to manufacture – about three average working lifetimes. Total production ran to more than 20,000 in two dozen major marks. This aircraft is the RAF Battle of Britain Memorial Flight's Mark Vb

A rear view mirror and a constantly swivelling neck were vital life preservers in WW II dogfights

Below Is there a sweeter sound? For warbird fans, there is probably no note better than that of a Rolls-Royce Merlin . . . except perhaps two Merlins, or three, or . . .

Right Somewhere in England, 1940? Booker Airfield, near High Wycombe, 1984. Christie's director The Honourable Patrick Lindsay's Spitfire 1A awaits an overhauled propeller ready for the airshow season. Lindsay's aeroplane is one of five Mark I Spits in England, but the only airworthy example in the world. Only die-hard purists would carp that its propeller should have three, and not four blades

The stuff small boys (and some big ones) dream of: a Spitfire cockpit. Huge spade grip on the 'joystick' was hinged for lateral control, while the whole column moved fore and aft for pitch inputs. The thumb switch at top left of the grip fired the guns

Above Throttle quadrant, propeller pitch control and elevator trim wheel on the port side of the cockpit, quaintly named 'chassis' lever for raising and lowering the undercarriage to starboard. RAF groundcrews imposed their own system of fines on careless pilots who damaged aircraft and caused them extra work. Forget to lower your chassis and £5 went into the repair crew's beer fund. Today such a piece of sacrilege would cost you rather more

Conceived as a lightweight redesign of the Tempest, the Hawker Fury was rejected by the RAF and adapted for shipboard service with the Fleet Air Arm as the Sea Fury, powered by a 2550 hp Bristol Centaurus 18-cylinder sleeve-valve engine driving a five-bladed propeller. Roughly equivalent to the US Navy's Bearcat, though rather more stable as a gun platform, the Sea Fury saw action during the Korean War and is credited with the destruction of a MiG-15 when a Communist pilot strayed within range of No 802 Sqn Fleet Air Arm pilot Lt Peter Carmichael's four 20 mm cannon. The Sea Fury at left belonged to the late Ormond Haydon-Baillie and is painted in RAF colours as a Fury. Haydon-Baillie raced the stock unmodified Sea Fury at Reno in the 1970s while serving with the Royal Canadian Air Force, subsequently bringing it to England. He died in the crash of a Cavalier Mustang while giving an aerobatic performance in Germany

Above Two seat Sea Fury T.20 was a trainer version

The Fleet Air Arm Historic Flight's Sea Fury FB.11 served in the Korean War with No 807 Sqn aboard the aircraft carrier HMS *Theseus*, flying 200 operational sorties before retirement in 1954. Manufacturers Hawkers gave the aircraft back to the Royal Navy in 1971 for complete restoration to airworthiness. It carries authentic markings worn during the Korean campaign. The Sea Fury was the last of the Fleet Air Arm's propeller driven fighters and with a maximum speed in full military trim of 460 mph, lays claim to being the fastest production single-engined piston fighter. Stripped Sea Furies in racing trim have exceeded 520 mph in the United States. The complexities of the sleeve-valve Centaurus engine have inspired several conversions to more familiar (to Americans at least) Pratt & Whitney radials

Overleaf Californian Frank Sanders flew this Sea Fury T.20 fitted with wingtip smoke generators for airshow work

Frank Sanders not only paints pretty pictures in the
sky with his smoke-belching Sea Fury, but uses the
aeroplane to give graphic demonstrations of the dangers
of wingtip vortices. Sanders has re-engined a two-seat
Sea Fury with a 4000 hp Pratt & Whitney R-4360-28
'corn cob' engine. Named *Dreadnought*, and flown by
General Dynamics test pilot Neil Anderson who is
more usually seen in the sci-fi cockpit of an F-16
Fighting Falcon, the Sea Fury won the 1983 Reno
Unlimited Class championship at a race speed of 425
mph

Wings and wires. Shiny Tiger Moth being put to bed at the end of a summer's day was owned by an American F-111 pilot stationed in England and wears the markings of a 1930s RAF Central Flying School formation aerobatic team, an early forerunner of the Red Arrows. Ancient double-decker bus in the background is the headquarters of a gliding club

Above and Overleaf The Fairey Swordfish torpedo bomber was an anachronism when WW II broke out, yet served courageously throughout the conflict and outlasted its intended successor. Popularly known as the Stringbag, not for its bestrutted, wire-braced airframe, but because it could carry 'more stores than a lady could fit into her stringbag on a shopping trip', the unlikely looking biplane was responsible for sinking a greater tonnage of enemy shipping in WW II than any other Allied aircraft. This example is the only airworthy Swordfish, flown regularly by the Fleet Air Arm Historic Flight. The 'torpedo' is a dummy, doubling as a handy baggage container for airshow trips away from its base at RNAS Yeovilton, Somerset. For the benefit of those who might wonder, the author can confirm that the Stringbag's open cockpit is c-o-l-d,

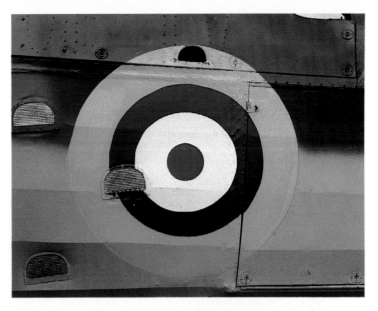

even on a balmy Somerset spring day. Imagine what it must have been like operating off a carrier in winter up near the Arctic Circle. Or perhaps you would rather not

To the Army they were T-6s. The Navy called theirs
SNJs. Brits and Canucks preferred Harvard.
Whichever, the North American trainer was an exciting
prospect for trainee pilots: 550 hp, retractable
undercarriage, not too difficult to imagine yourself in
one of the fighters on the recruiting posters. Rookie
pilots training under the Commonwealth Air Training
Plan moved up to Harvards after 65 hours flying on
Tiger Moth or Fleet Finch biplanes. The USAAC used
their AT-6s for advanced training, but eventually
dispensed with the 'A' designation and used the aircraft
for basic instruction, putting new recruits straight into
the T-6's big cockpit. The bright yellow Harvard at
left in Royal Canadian Air Force colours is owned by
Len Fallowfield of Ontario

Above Navy SNJ-5 (note the arrestor hook) belongs to
Warbirds of America director Jerry Walbrun, who
regularly leads airshow formations of up to 32 T-
6s/SNJs/Harvards. The buzz-saw rasp of all those
Wasp engines and the howl of near supersonic
propeller tips which characterize the aircraft is pure
heaven for some, sheer masochism for anti-noise
campaigners

Military colour schemes are not essential for T-6s, but few owners can resist the temptation to give their birds a warlike appearance. These two aircraft are British owned, one in USAAF colours, the other, right, in RAF wartime trainer camouflage. Surplus T-6s have appeared on the civilian market in large numbers in recent years as the smaller European air forces finally replace them with modern trainers

Tight formation take-off by a pair of T-6s at the EAA convention at Oshkosh. The aircraft nearest the camera is a remanufactured T-6G, some 700 of which were updated from earlier marks in 1950 with new clear-vision canopies, increased fuel tankage and upgraded instrumentation. Some were used during the Korean War as forward air control spotters, directing air strikes against North Korean positions

Good forward vision was not a T-6 strongpoint, so trainees had to remember to weave from side to side while taxying, rudders waggling like ducks' tails.
Left More than a few inadvertently sawed the tail off the T-6 ahead

Leader Jerry Walbrun calls for the landing break as the first gaggle of T-6s peel off to enter the pattern after a Warbirds of America T-6 spectacular. Viewed from the ground it looks just a trifle scary; from the cockpit of one of the aircraft the manoeuvre has a high pucker/white knuckle factor for back-seat riders

Two rare machines. Left, mirror-bright aluminium aglow in the sunset is John and Susan Harrison's early model AT-6A, the fifth of its type built. The 1940 aircraft was completely restored over three years by the Sacramento-based couple and took the EAA Grand Champion Warbird Trophy at Oshkosh in 1977. Markings are those of a flight-check trainer with the 94th Hat-in-Ring Pursuit Squadron based at Selfridge Field, Michigan

Above Californians Dennis Buehn and Randy Difani used a Canadian Harvard airframe to recreate this North American BC-2 basic combat trainer prototype of 1939. Major surgery included the installation of a geared Pratt & Whitney R-1340 engine driving a three-bladed propeller, extended cowling, control surface gap seals, new rudder, wing incidence reduction and an extensive weight reduction programme

The outer limits

The North American T-28 was the T-6's successor,
serving with the USAF, US Navy and Marine Corps
as a basic and instrument trainer from 1950 onwards.
Power comes from an 800 hp Wright R-1300 seven
cylinder radial engine. Huge bubble canopy provides
superb cockpit visibility. The T-28B at left is finished
in the blue and gold colours of the US Navy's *Blue
Angels* flight demonstration team for reasons best
known to owner J M Ellis III, since the Blues never
operated the aircraft. Bob Urbine's yellow bird is ex-
USAF T-28A upgraded to T-28D standard

The US Navy ordered 489 T-28Bs in 1952 and three years later came back for another 299 T-28Cs which had strengthened landing gear, smaller diameter propellers and arrestor hooks for operations from training carriers for pilot deck landing qualification. This restored (and for sale) example wears the yellow training colours of Navy squadron VT-2 which operated T-28Bs from NAS Whiting Field until the late 1970s when they were replaced by Beech T-34C Turbo Mentors. However, the large diameter nosewheel and high profile canopy suggests that the aircraft is an impostor, probably an ex-USAF T-28A/D

T-28s were widely exported to overseas customers
following their withdrawal from the US military
inventory. Latin America, some African nations and
France were major recipients, as was the South
Vietnamese Air Force whose colours are worn by this
T-28D

Dave Schwartz's aggressive T-28 is a C model, formerly a US Navy trainer restored in the colours of the South Vietnamese Air Force's 1st Air Commando unit. Gun pods, rockets, 500 lb bombs and napalm were carried by VNAF T-28s between 1963–65, but the aircraft suffered heavily from ground fire and structural failures and were eventually replaced with A-1H Skyraiders

All teeth, but not much bite. The Fairchild PT-26 was
strictly non-combatant as a WW II primary trainer,
powered by a 200 hp Ranger L-440-3 inline engine.
The aircraft evolved from the similar, but lower
powered PT-19 of 1940, and was used by the US
Army Air Corps and Royal Canadian Air Force, who
called theirs the Cornell

In 1938 the Cessna Aircraft Company was a low-volume producer of single-engined lightplanes when design work was started on the T-50 twin-engined light transport. Its selection by the Royal Canadian Air Force as a multi-engine trainer for the Empire Air Training scheme gave Cessna its first major order – for 640 aircraft, more than twice the total manufactured by the Wichita company in 12 years of business – and set Cessna up as one of the world's leading lightplane manufacturers. More than 5500 T-50s were built, most of them as Cranes for the RCAF or AT-17 bomber trainers and UC-78 utility transports for the USAAC. The big round cowlings house a pair of 245 hp Jacobs R-755 engines, popularly known as Shaky Jakes for their less than smooth running. The aircraft was

officially dubbed Bobcat by the US military, but attracted many less complimentary nicknames of which *Bamboo Bomber*, *Double Breasted Cub* and *Useless 78* are the most kind

The Stearman training biplane was one of the few
things the US Army and Navy ever agreed upon. Both
services ordered the aircraft in the mid-1930s and used
it as a primary trainer throughout WW II.
Paradoxically Lloyd Stearman played no part in the
design of the classic American biplane which bears his
name; he left the Wichita company in 1932, two years
before designers Harold Zipp and Jack Clark unveiled
their first Stearman Model 70 from which the Army
PT-13/17 and Navy N2Ss evolved. 10,346 Stearmans
were built. This handsome specimen is restored as a
Navy N2S-5, powered by a 225 hp Lycoming R680
engine

Ask an American to name a light aeroplane and the chances are he will say Piper Cub. But when some J-3 Cubs took part in the 1941 Third Army Manoeuvres at El Paso, Texas, a sceptical cavalry brigade commander was moved to observe that they 'looked like goddammed grasshoppers out in the boondocks.' Thus the 6000 Cubs ordered by the US Army were known, like this one, as Grasshoppers, but more properly designated L-4s. Grasshoppers (readily identifiable by their extended greenhouse canopies) served in all major theatres of war up to Korea, performing liaision and artillery spotting duties from fields, roads, launching platforms atop tank landing craft and during the capture of Okinawa, from a cable strung between stanchions on landing ships. Burning four gallons of fuel an hour on 65 hp the Cub/Grasshopper is an economic warbird. As comedian Bob Hope put it, 'a P-51 that wouldn't eat its cereal'

Below and Overleaf Successful winner of a contest to find a replacement for the North American T-6 in the USAF inventory, Beechcraft's T-34 Mentor served as a basic trainer with the USAF and US Navy, and was licence manufactured in Japan by Fuji Industries. The example pictured right is a Wichita-built Mentor, restored to Japanese Self Defence Force colours. The highly buffed T-34A overleaf bears the colours of the Special Air Missions wing of the USAF which

transports VIPs including incumbents of the White House. Presidents and First Ladies do not travel in single-engine trainers, however, though SAM crews might have used T-34s for refresher training or routine travel – callsign *Air Force Point One*, perhaps?

Right A contemporary of the Stearman, the Naval Aircraft Factory N3N was manufactured by the US Navy's own plant at the Philadelphia Navy Yard. It was unusual in having a bolted steel tube fuselage with removable metal panels for ease of maintenance access. N3Ns served in primary training schools throughout WW II. A few, equipped with floats, were retained by the US Naval Academy for training midshipmen as late as 1961, the last biplanes to see military service following the USAF's disposal of its Stearmans in 1948. This aircraft is an N3N-3, powered by a 235 hp Wright R-760-2 radial engine

White star, red star. Walter Beech's Model 17 biplane, colloquially known as the Staggerwing because of its unusual negative-stagger wing arrangement, was as fast as the latest US military pursuit aircraft when the first models appeared in 1932, and is one of the most sought after antiques, with 200 mph cruise speed and a roomy cabin seating five. In wartime Staggerwings were used by the USAAF, US Navy and British Fleet Air Arm for communications duties and VIP transport. This 450 hp Pratt & Whitney Wasp-powered Beechcraft has been restored by Staggerwing buff Glenn McNabb of Jasper, Tennessee in the Navy colours it wore during wartime service as a GB-2

Below 'You do not have a YAK,' Soviet officials told British aircraft restorer Doug Bianchi when he asked them for help in rebuilding this Russian YAK-11 trainer rescued from a dump after a forced landing on the island of Cyprus. Oh yes he did, and what's more he completed the rebuild without their help. The YAK later caused a stir at a USAF base in Britain when the late Neil Williams was forced to land unannounced with an engine problem, and is now resident in the United States. Happy juxtaposition of Soviet marks and stars and stripes provides an inadvertent East-West confrontation which the photographer did not intend

Military Stearmans were known as Kaydets, though the orange-yellow navy ships were popularly dubbed Yellow Perils, because of their colour and the knowledge that they were flown by neophyte aviators who needed plenty of air room. Here a restored US Army PT-17 and US Navy N2S-2 share a common patch at the EAA Oshkosh fly-in

Above Another Navy Peril, this rare Timm N2T-1 Tutor featured a patented form of plastic-bonded-plywood construction called Aeromold which resulted in a very smooth, drag-free surface giving more performance per horsepower than contemporary wood or fabric-skinned trainers. Some 260 were built from 1943 for the US Navy, but only four are known to survive in airworthy condition

The Stinson L-5 was the US Army's flying jeep in WW II and Korea. Its STOL capabilities and high stall/spin resistance enabled the L-5 to operate from tiny airstrips which few other types could get into in pre-helicopter days. A Marine Corps OY-1 variant was the first aircraft to land on Iwo Jima after the Americans took the island from the Japanese

Left Huge glasshouse cabin and wide doors make the L-5 a superb camera ship. This aircraft, finished in the markings of the 13th Air Force operating out of the Philippines in WW II is off on a photo sortie at Oshkosh

The US Navy received 423 Beech T-34B Mentor primary trainers between 1954–57. This one is a privately owned aircraft in 1950s chrome yellow Navy trainer colours. Few piston-engined Mentors remain in service with the US Navy, having been superceded by the Pratt & Whitney PT-6 turbine-engined T-34C Turbo Mentor

Overleaf Temco's TE-1B Buckaroo vied for the USAF contract won by the Beech Mentor. Less than 20 were built, including ten for the Saudi Arabian Air Force and one each for Italy and Israel. This immaculate restoration of a USAF YT-35 is one of two surviving in the United States, owned by Californian Len Lundmark

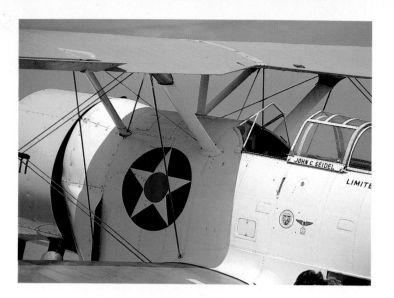

You can see why the Grumman J2F Duck amphibian was dubbed *the flying boot*. The 1933 design served pre-war with the US Navy and US Coast Guard as an observation and utility aircraft, and was resurrected during WW II when the Navy ordered a further 330 aircraft. Grumman was fully committed on fighter projects, so these Ducks, designated J2F-6s, were built by Columbia Aircraft Corporation at Valley Stream, Long Island. John Seidel's Duck is one of them, powered by a 900 hp Wright R-1820-54 engine and finished here in attractive, though for the J2F-6, inappropriate pre-Pearl Harbor US Navy colours with large neutrality star

US Army flight cadets graduated from PT-17 Stearmans or Fairchild PT-19/26s onto the Vultee BT-13 before they were let loose on AT-6s. Officially known as the Valiant, any BT-13 trained pilot will tell you the aeroplane's real name: *Vibrator*, because the 450 hp Pratt & Whitney Wasp-engined trainer was noted for the all over massage job it provided in flight. More than 11,000 were built, but few survive in flying condition, and many of those that have were converted into replica Japanese Kate and Val torpedo bombers for movie roles

Neat cowl job on the 160 hp Kinner radial engine and 'elbow' jointed undercarriage legs characterize the Ryan PT-22 Recruit primary trainer which joined the US Army Air Corps in 1942. 1023 were built for the Army and Navy. The aircraft was developed from the civilian ST series of two-seat trainers and aerobatic aircraft which had Menasco inline engines. The PT-22 had swept back wings (a modest four degrees and barely noticeable in these photographs), roomier cockpits to accomodate pilots in full military flight gear, and lacked the undercarriage 'trouser' fairings of the civilian variants

Above and Overleaf *Pop-pop-pop* goes the Kinner, forever sounding as if it is only running on four of its five cylinders. Despite the external wire bracing the PT-22 was among the fastest primary trainers, cruising around 120 mph, and is renowned for its sprightly snap-rolls, not always entirely voluntary on the part of its pilots

Right and Overleaf Only ten Stearman Model 6s were built in 1930–31. Four went to the US Army for evaluation as primary trainers to replace fleets of ageing Curtiss Jennies. This one was built as a civilian Model 6L with 170 hp Continental A.70 radial engine, was later upgraded to 6L standard with a 200 hp Lycoming R-680, and was discovered derelict in a cropduster's hangar with another of its rare kind in the early 1960s by Californians Ray Stephen and Darrel Hansen. Meticulous restoration job on both aircraft saw this one (overleaf) emerge as a US Army YPT-9B Cloudbody. Not surprisingly the Stearman won the 1967 Antique Airplane Associaton of America's Grand Champion award

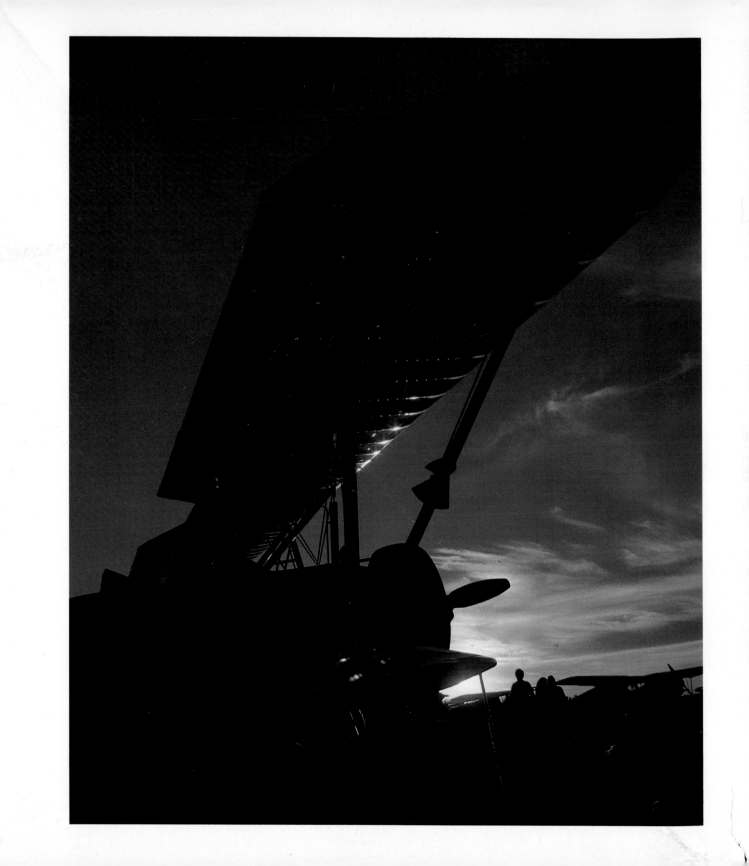